SEEDS

Of

REVIVAL

BY

Ruth Shinness–Brinduse

Printed by
Evangel Press
Nappanee, IN

WHY THIS COVER ?
WE CAN WALK IN THE REVIVAL LIFE BY THE POWER OF GOD WHEN WE CHOOSE TO GO THE "WAY OF THE CROSS". THIS BOOK TELLS HOW THIS CAN HAPPEN.

FRONT COVER

Elevation of the Cross, circa 1620, by John Paul Rubens on a large mural in a church in Antwerp. The church burned down destroying the mural.
All that was left was a sketch Rubens made in preparation for the painting.
Artist Michael G. Miller found out about the sketch, now hanging in the Louvre, and made a large painting 50" x 58" oil and canvas. This is a copy of it. Web: michaelgmillerfineart.net email: mgmfineart@gmail.com

To obtain additional copies of this material, look at back page.

ISBN 978-0-9821186-1-0
Cover Artist: Jasmine Shininess jazzi@tomshinness.com

FORWARD

INTERCESSORS 2009:

Have gone from
A deep burden for our country
To a lively expectation.

GOD IS SAYING:

"I am still the leader."

INTERCESSORS SAY:

God is causing them to pray more,
Sharpening their skills in prayer.
They are worshiping God more.
They are having more joy in prayer.
They feel more of His presence.

A WHOLE NEW SPIRIT

Is blowing on God's people of prayer.

IN THE MIDST OF TRIALS

In our country,
God is awaking His people
To a new day of His presence
Where there is fullness of joy.

THE COMMON PERSON

Will be anointed to minister to others
In a way never known before
Except in the early church.

YES, WE WILL HAVE SUFFERINGS

But God will turn our sufferings into testimonies.
That will cause others to believe,
And they shall "taste and see that the Lord is good".

Habakkuk 3:17-19 NKJV Though the fig tree may not blossom. Nor fruit be on the vines; though the labor of the olive may fail. And the field yield no food: Though the flock may be cut off from the fold, and there be no herd in the stalls – Yet I will rejoice in the Lord, I will joy in the God of my salvation. The Lord God is my strength, He will make my feet like deer's feet. And He will make me walk on my high hills.

TABLE OF CONTENTS

Dedication Page……………………………………..………..2

Forward……………………………………… ……...….3

IF MY PEOPLE, WHICH ARE CALLED BY MY NAME

What Is This Book About?……………………………….....7

Looking At God's People…………………………...…......8

Famine of the Word………………………………………..10

Prayer Movement Today……………………………......12

God's Purpose in Suffering…….……………………..……14

Summary, If My People, Which Are Called By My Name.16

SHALL HUMBLE THEMSELVES AND PRAY

First Prayer Strategy……..……………………...……....18

Testing During Trials..……………………………………20

Second Prayer Strategy……………………………..…..22

We Receive Our Answers to Prayer……….……………...24

Third Prayer Strategy……………………………….……..26

Summary: Shall Humble Themselves and Pray…………...28

AND SEEK MY FACE

Learning Focus in Prayer…………………………..……...30

How Do We Fight the Battle?……..………………….…...32

Hearing God's Voice Individually…..……………………34

Hearing God's Voice in a Group…..…………….……...36

Summary: And Seek My Face……………………………..38

AND TURN FROM THEIR WICKED WAYS

Seeking Revival for Ourselves…………………………...….40

Other Books of Influence.......................................42

The "Lost" Page.......................................44

Sin Revealed Leads to Revival 46

Women Can Be Key to the Answer.......................................48

Praying for Troubled Families.......................................50

Caring for the Unloving.......................................52

Woman Without Hope: Victory.......................................54

Children Changing: Homes Now Peaceful.......................................56

Rhonda's Story.......................................58

Summary: And Turn From Their Wicked Ways.......................................60

THEN WILL I HEAR FROM HEAVEN - CHURCH

Revival in the Church.......................................62

Church Blockages.......................................64

Summary: Revival In The Church.......................................60

FORGIVE THEIR SINS AND HEAL THEIR LAND

Praying for Our Country.......................................68

Praying for Our Leaders.......................................70

How to Win the Victory.......................................72

DAILY PRAYERS FOR COUNTRY

Prayers: Victory Over the Enemy.......................................74

Prayers: Prayers for Those in Authority.......................................76

Prayers: Bringing Unity.......................................78

RESOURCES

Books and Resources.......................................80

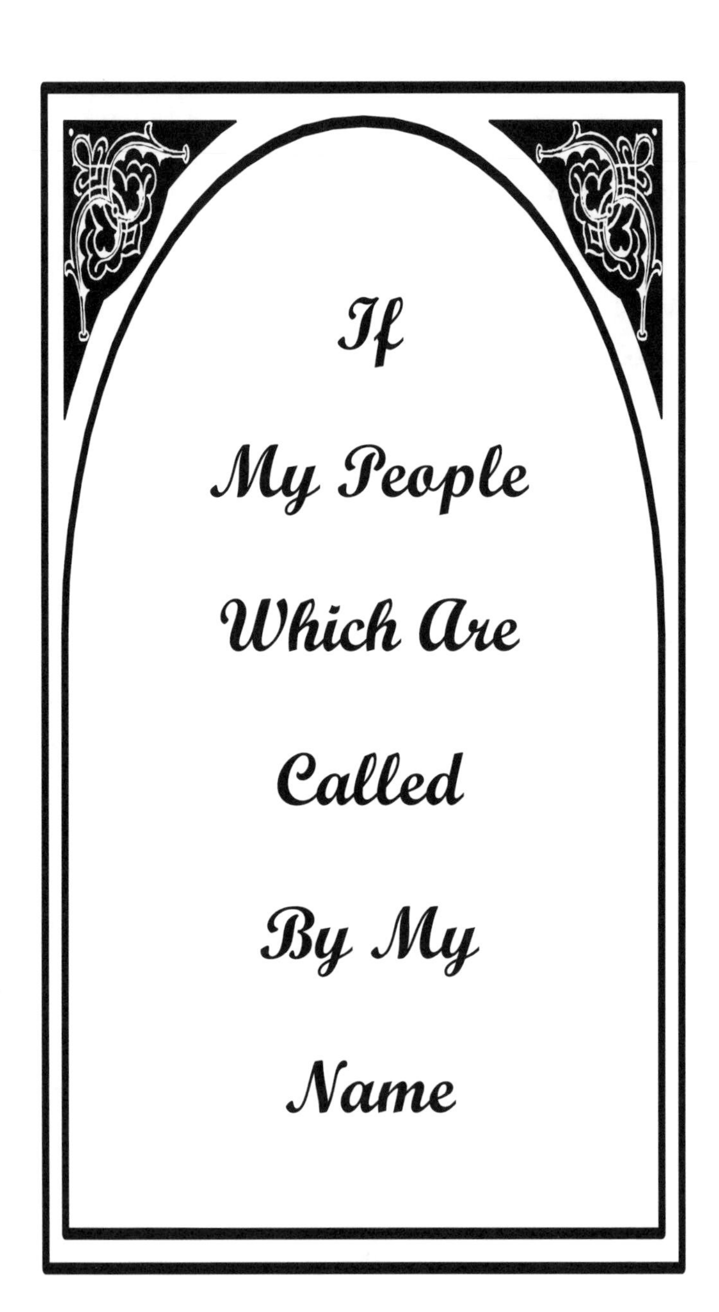
If
My People
Which Are
Called
By My
Name

WHAT THIS BOOK IS ABOUT

II Chronicles 7:14 If my people, which are called by my name, shall humble themselves, and pray, and seek my face, and turn from their wicked ways; then will I hear from heaven, and will forgive their sin, and will heal their land.

REVIVAL STARTS WITH GOD'S PEOPLE:

We are the ones who have to change first.
We can plant these Seeds Of Revival *i*n our own lives.

SEED: IF MY PEOPLE WHO ARE CALLED BY MY NAME:

Where we learn to change,
We change the environment around us,
Whether it is in our home, our church or our nation.

SEED: WILL HUMBLE THEMSELVES AND PRAY:

Many of us have prayed much
But have not seen very many answers.
Now we will learn to pray with
Simple effective skills that produce results,
Activating the Word of God
To bring God's plan to pass.

SEED: AND SEEK MY FACE:

What does that mean?
How can we hear His voice?
Does this mean Worship?
Being in His presence?

SEED: AND TURN FROM OUR WICKED WAYS:

Learning how sin is hidden
In our human natural person;
Shining the light on what that means.

THEN GOD HEARS FROM HEAVEN:

He is ready to give us what became ours
When Jesus died on the cross.

AND HEALS OUR LAND:

God Himself coming in His power
And we experience Him as our REVIVAL,
Our joy unspeakable and full of Glory!

IF MY PEOPLE, WHICH ARE CALLED BY MY NAME

LOOKING AT GOD'S PEOPLE

In the Old Testament,
Showing God's pattern
So we as Christians
Will know what pleases God
And what does not please God.

<u>Deut. 28:2</u> And all these blessings shall come on thee and overtake thee, if thou shall harken unto the voice of thy Lord thy God.

GOD CHOSE THE JEWS,

Set them apart, put His love upon them.
He prospered them; they would lend and not borrow.

GOD WOULD FIGHT THEIR ENEMIES FOR THEM.

Whatever they did would be blessed.
He would bless their children.
He would make them a holy people.
They would be the head and not the tail.
They would have good crops.

THAT SOUNDS LIKE AMERICA.

Our foundation was God,
Putting Him first, honoring Him,
Doing what was right in God's eyes.
And God blessings have been upon us.

WHEN ISRAEL DID RIGHT, GOD BLESSED THEM.

When they did not do right in His eyes,
He would send an enemy to destroy them or
Famine or pestilence or fire and brimstone.

WHAT IS IT THAT GOD WANTED?

First He wanted to be loved, honored
And to be their only God.
He wanted to be worshiped.
He didn't want to be left out.
He wanted them to do what He said.

NO SEXUAL SINS

No sex outside of marriage.
In fact, the Jews were to kill
Anyone caught in sexual sin.
Does that give you an idea what
God thinks?

IF SOMEONE MURDERED,

God instructed
They would be put to death.

THE BIBLE SAYS

The fear of the Lord is
The beginning of wisdom.
How do we get the fear of the Lord?
By finding out what God wants
Through reading the Bible
So we will be afraid of not pleasing God,
When we read what God did to Israel
When they disobeyed.

AMERICA HAS BEEN BLESSED

But in many of our churches,
We do not know what the Bible says
Nor do we understand what God does to
Those who do not do His ways.

3,000 BABIES MURDERED

By their own mothers each day
Without hardly a word form the pulpit.
We have let homosexuality spring up
Without a murmur from us Christians.
How many sermons have you heard on these issues? Zero?

NOW THE ENEMY HAS COME IN LIKE A FLOOD

At last we have the Fear of the Lord on us.
But all is not hopeless
I will be sharing how we as God's people
Can raise up a standard against the enemy
In our own personal lives
And in the life of our church and country.

WE ARE WILLING

But how could this happen?

A FAMINE OF THE WORD

In the last days, the Bible says
There will be a famine of the Word of God,
But we have so many churches in USA,
How could that be?

ATTENDANCE IS DOWN

Could it be that there is a famine of the Word
And we don't know it?

EVEN THOUGH WE ARE ALL FOR THE WORD

Are we really reading through the Bible?

WHEN WE READ THROUGH THE BIBLE

Then the Fear of the Lord comes upon us.

WHAT IS THE FEAR OF LORD?

It is the beginning of Wisdom.
Wisdom to know that if we do
What God says, He will bless us.
Knowing that if we do not do what He says,
He will chastise us.

WHEN ISRAEL WAS NOT

Following God's Word,
Even though faithful to attend Temple meetings,
Then everyone did what they thought
Was right in their own eyes.
They were *for* what God was *against*.

SINCE WE GO TO CHURCH,

We accept the Word, believe the Word,
But few read the Word
For themselves.

PEOPLE ARE SO BUSY

They don't have time to read the Bible
Or just have a five-minute devotion in the morning,
Or leave out the Old Testament altogether.
It's not relevant for today, they think.

NOW IN OUR COUNTRY,

There is a famine of the Word of God —
Christians doing what is right in their own eyes.

CHRISTIANS VOTING FOR LEADERS

Who are *for* what God is *against*.
It sounds soooo good to some.
Leaders say, "I will give you……"
But is soooo bad in God's eyes.

DO YOU THINK WE ARE SEEING

The results of our choices?
Are we now finally bothered
By what is happening in our country?

RUTH READ THROUGH THE BIBLE

Every year for a number of years.
She likes the Bibles that have
A reading each day for Old Testament,
Psalms, Proverbs, New Testament.

PEOPLE SAY THEY DON'T HAVE TIME.

You have to make it a priority, it can be done.

RUTH MARRIED DAN IN 2003

She had no time to pray and read Bible; her ministry was growing. Ruth was enjoying her time with Dan.

RUTH WAS SPEAKING IN KENYA,

She had lunch with guests in the dining room.
Joyce Myers was speaking on TV in the living room.

RUTH COULD HEAR HER, BUT NOT WORDS.

Suddenly the voices around the table faded.
Ruth could hear their voices at the table but not their words.

LIVING ROOM SOUNDS

Like someone turned up the TV.
Ruth could hear Joyce's words.

JOYCE SAID: WHEN HER MINISTRY GREW,

She didn't have time to pray and read the Word.
The Lord said: "If you don't give Me prayer time
And Bible time like you did before, I will not
Grow your ministry anymore."
Voices around the table became normal; Joyce's faded.

RUTH GOT THE MESSAGE.

Back to her # 1 priority.

PRAYER MOVEMENT TODAY

WHY I THINK GOD WANTS TO

Do something great in our country?
Because He has more people of prayer
In the USA than any other time in our history.

IN CITIES ALL OVER OUR COUNTRY

Interdenominational prayer groups
Have sprung up praying for Revival.

WHEN GOD WANTED TO DO SOMETHING SPECIAL,

He would raise up people to pray.
How did this prayer movement start?

CHURCHES WHO ARE STRONG

In the Word of God,
As they read their Bibles,
The fear of the Lord comes upon them,
For they read what God did to countries that sinned.
And America is in line for God's judgment.

ANOTHER AREA: CHARISMATIC MOVEMENT

God started to fill people
All over the world with the Holy Spirit.
He touched people in denominational churches,
Catholic churches and the un-churched.

WHAT HAPPENED TO THESE PEOPLE?

They wanted to pray, read their Bibles.
Their understanding was opened to the Bible.
God touched their lives so they had a testimony and
Power to witness to others.

NO WONDER JESUS SAID TO WAIT IN JERUSALEM

Until they received this power.
It was to be part of their equipment as Christians.

MILLIONS OF CHURCHES WERE RAISED UP

All over the world when the Holy Spirit came.

Luke 24:49 NKJV (Jesus said) Behold I send the promise of my father unto you; but tarry in the city of Jerusalem until you are endued with "power from on high." Acts 2:4a NKJV (in Jerusalem) And they were all filled with the Holy Spirit.

THE BIBLE SAID IN THAT DAY THEY WILL SAY,

"Praise the Lord," and that happened.
That is just what they said.
And we guessed
The Holy Spirit had come to them. Amazing!!!!!

SONGS OF PRAISE TO GOD CAME FORTH

That are sung in churches all over the world.
These people wanted to worship.
These songs are sung in most all churches today.

I THINK THIS MOVE OF GOD

Was brought forth for a time like this
So God would have a people
Who know what the Bible says,
What God likes, and
What God does not like.

RUTH SPEAKS TO PEOPLE OF PRAYER.

God is helping them pray more.
They are seeing answers more quickly.
They are having better prayer skills.
They are praising God more.
There is more reality of God's presence.

WEDNESDAY PRAYER GROUP, HAMILTON, OH

Praying all day every Wednesday
For 47 years in Presbyterian Church.
They now pray Prayer Strategy Resource Book
And get more answers to prayer.
After all those years of praying,
They like what works.

THE LORD TOLD THEM EACH TO PRAY

Three pages from the Prayer Strategy Resource Book,
"Praying For Those in Authority" page,
"Bringing Unity" page, and
"Victory Over the Enemy" page
Each day, changing wording to "For Our Country"
And they would see the results.
(I have added these pages at the end of this book.)

GOD'S PURPOSE IN SUFFERING

ISRAEL TURNED AWAY FROM GOD.

The Lord told them,
"I will prosper you, give you everything,
Then you will not need Me anymore
And you will turn away from Me and My ways."

THEN GOD BROUGHT SUFFERING TO THEM,

Enemies to defeat them. They burned their cities,
Took them into captivity and made them slaves.

THEN FINALLY THEY WOKE UP

And decided to turn back to God
And do what pleased Him
So God could bless them once more.

GOD IS CHASTISING OUR NATION

The economy is ruined,
Government is being taken over
By godless Socialism,
A flood of sin is flowing through our country.

MANY ARE ALREADY SUFFERING

Loss of work and homes,
Savings disappearing
Before their eyes.

HOW MUCH CHASTISEMENT

Will we suffer before we
Turn back to God and go His way?

THE PLACE OF SUFFERING

There are sufferings that come
That draw us closer to God;
That mould our character;
That make us more loving.

RUTH WENT THROUGH SUFFERINGS

When a loved one lost his way.
It made her draw closer to God.
It made her search the scriptures
For better ways to pray.

SUFFERING MADE HER PRAY MORE,

Giving up TV, less time shopping,
Other time wasting, non-productive things
That did not produce the answers she wanted.

GOD CALLED RUTH TO STAY HOME

Just go when her husband went.
This would last for 25 years.

SUFFERING CAN BE YOUR FRIEND

When it presses you to God.
The drawing closer to God
Gave Ruth a testimony of answered prayer
As she learned new prayer skills
That have encouraged many people
All around the world to believe God for their answers.

PEOPLE WHO GET THE MOST OUT OF

Ruth's Prayer Strategies are the ones who are suffering
And they see that this way of prayer works.
They are desperate enough to spend time praying.

RUTH WOULD NOT HAVE A MINISTRY

If she had not gone through suffering.
God still gives Ruth burdens, close to her heart,
But now Ruth has learned to turn these burdens
Into worship and praise for the answers
She sees in the Prayer Strategy Resource Book.

You have given me a new song to sing of praise unto You, my God. Now many hear the glorious things You have done for me, and stand in awe before You, and put their trust in You. Psalms 40:3 TLB He has given me a new song to sing of praises to our God. Now many will hear the glorious things He has done for me and stand in awe before the Lord and put their trust in Him

COULD IT BE.......

That the dark things that are happening to people
In our country today
Could turn into testimonies?

I BELIEVE THAT COULD HAPPEN

As suffering turns to joy.

IF MY PEOPLE, WHICH ARE CALLED BY MY NAME

REVIVAL SEED # 1

RECAP: EQUIPPING GOD'S PEOPLE FOR REVIVAL

1. LOOKING AT GOD'S PEOPLE

a. What God wanted His people Israel to do.
b. What He did not want them to do.
c What happened to Israel.
d. What is happening to USA today.

2 A FAMINE OF THE WORD OF GOD

a. No time to read the Bible.
b. No time for God.
c. Without reading the Bible, we do what is right in our own eyes. Sin comes in.

3. PRAYER MOVEMENT TODAY

a. More people of prayer in USA than ever before.
b. People pray from churches who know God's Word.
c. Holy Spirit comes, people want to pray and read Bible more.
d. When God wants to bring revival, He raises up people to pray.
e. God's plan: to yet bless us.

4. GOD'S PURPOSE IN SUFFERING

a. To bring us to Him.
b. So we will need Him.
c. So we will do what He wants.
d. So He can bless us.
e. So we can experience revival.

Summary: Gods people need to know what He wants. They will know what He wants if they read the Bible. They need to be equipped with the Holy Spirit so they will want to pray, read the Bible, and be on fire for God. People will suffer in USA, causing many to seek God. Then Revival!

Shall
Humble
Themselves
And
Pray

FIRST PRAYER STRATEGY

RUTH STAYED HOME TO RAISE A FAMILY,
Felt all would go well if she did this.
She wanted to be with her children as they grew up.

SHE WANTED TO HAVE TIME WITH HER HUSBAND
Have a meal on the table when he got home,
Build a good friendship with him.

THEY HAD VERY LITTLE MONEY
But God provided their needs.
They thought the people in the home
More important than material things.
Results? Happy home – good marriage.

RUTH WAS A PERSON TO PRAY.
She read books on prayer; loved to read testimonies;
Tried different ways of prayer.

RUTH AND HUSBAND LES
Went to church and prayed many hours.
They saw very few answers.

SHE PRAYED WITH CITY REVIVAL PRAYER GROUP
Where are the answers?
E-mails came telling what to pray for
But never told the answers.

RUTH WOULD READ THROUGH THE BIBLE
One to three times a year.
Doing all this, yet where were the results?

ONE OF HER CHILDREN WITH PROBLEMS:
Ruth was all prayed out; she had no strength left;
Just pain and misery.
Would she ever feel good again?

"LORD, I KNOW YOU'RE NOT BEING MEAN TO ME
By not answering my prayers.
There are secrets to getting results.
I don't know what they are
And I don't think anyone knows."

RUTH THOUGHT THESE SECRETS WERE HIDDEN

In the Word of God and she would search for them.

FIRST PRAYER STRATEGY

Ruth started going to a church
Where they taught her to pray the Word of God,
Reminding God of His promises.

Isaiah 62:6 Amp. I have set a watchman on your walls, O Jerusalem, who will never hold their peace day or night; you who [are His servants and by your prayers] put the Lord in remembrance [of His promises], keep not silence, and give Him no rest until He establishes Jerusalem and make it a praise in the earth.

THIS IS MORE THAN A FIVE MINUTE DEVOTIONAL

Never hold your peace?
Do this day and night, keep not silent?
Give Him no rest until He answers.
It is giving up "other" things to do this.

PASTOR DID NOT ALLOWED US TO SAY NEGATIVES

To each other, only to say the positive words
That lined up with the Word of God.

RUTH SAT IN THAT CHURCH SEVERAL MONTHS

Until hope seeped into her heart.
"Perhaps, all was not lost.
Could I be a winner after all?"

RUTH GOT A LITTLE LOOSE-LEAF NOTEBOOK

She thought, "What else do I want?"
As she read through the Bible,
She found topics of interest to her.

RUTH DEVELOPED PRAYER PAGES FOR

Children, Mother, Father,
Family, Prosper, Praise, Fear Not,
Success, Healing, and many more.

RUTH CARRIED THIS SCRIPTURE BOOK

Everywhere she went.
She walked with the book
By the hour, day after day,
Reminding God of His promises.

TESTINGS DURING TRIALS

RUTH DID NOT FEEL THE PRESENCE OF GOD.

Four-and-a-half years she prayed.
She did not get answers.
"God if I never get any answers,
If I never feel Your presence, I will still go after you."

WHAT MADE RUTH KEEP PRAYING?

Her suffering, her problems.
She was desperate for answers, she could not give up.

FOUR-AND-A-HALF YEARS LATER,

January 4, 1979, 2:00 AM,
There was a knock on her bedroom door.
Son said, "Mom and Dad, can I come in?
I want to get my life right with the Lord."

SON WENT ON TO BIBLE COLLEGE,

Graduated and they hired him
To teach music at the college.

WAS RUTH GLAD SHE DIDN'T GIVE UP?

You bet! She was glad -- full of joy.
Had she felt like giving up at times? Yes!

THEN RUTH STARTED TO GET MORE ANSWERS.

The fear left — she doesn't know when.
She received a healing.

FIRST PAGE OF PRAYER BOOK

Was for husband Les.
He was a great man, good to Ruth.
His unconditional love for her
Brought healing to her body
And joy to her heart.

WHAT DID RUTH WANT?

She wanted him to pray with her,
Study scriptures with her.
But he was very busy
With the business he owned.

ONE DAY LES CAME HOME SAYING

"The Lord has called me to
Sell my business, come home
Pray, fast and study scriptures."

THAT WAS NOT THE KIND OF ANSWER

Ruth had planned for.
How would they pay their bills?
What would they eat?
The answer to her prayer was shocking!

JANUARY 1, 1980, LES SOLD HIS BUSINESS,

Came home, wanted her by his side
To pray with Him and study scripture.

LES' GROUND RULES:

They would not ask for money
Or let anyone know their needs.
They would see if this was really God or not.

DID GOD PROVIDE ALL THEIR NEEDS? YES!

Were they tested? Yes!
One cold winter day,
The gas company was going to shut off their gas.
Ruth kept looking for the gas company truck.
It never came.

WHY DIDN'T THEY COME?

Because husband Les
Would give money to the gas company
In the winters for the poor who could not pay.
We were learning to trust in God. What a joy!

YES, THEY RAN OUT OF MONEY,

But they never missed a meal
They didn't plan to miss.
Someone gave them a freezer and God kept filling it up.
Ruth prayed the "Prosper" page.
ALL their needs were supplied.

WHAT AN ADVENTURE!

They were more thankful than ever before
For what they had and the food they ate.

<u>SECOND PRAYER STRATEGY</u>

IN 1991, LES HAD BYPASS SURGERY.

They had no health insurance and asked no one for money.
God worked and every bill was paid.

BUT, LES HAD BRAIN DAMAGE.

It was like Ruth had lost her best friend.
His speech was slurred, his balance was off.
He already was blind; his mind was not always working.

RUTH CAME INTO ANOTHER TIME OF SUFFERING

But also another **Prayer Strategy.**
Soon, she saw answers come more quickly.

IN HER PRAYER BOOK, RUTH HAD ALL

The New Testament scriptures on prayer.
She had prayed them with the other prayers
Expecting God would show her
The secrets of getting answers to prayer.

ONE DAY ONE OF THESE SCRIPTURES

Became big in her mind.

<u>Mark 11:24 NIV</u> Therefore I tell you, whatever you ask for in prayer, believe that you have received it, and it will be yours.

SHE HAD BEEN TAUGHT THIS SCRIPTURE

And she believed she was fulfilling that Word
But that day she realized she was not doing that.
She was not believing she **<u>now</u>** had the answer.

HOW WAS SHE PRAYING?

She was begging, pleading,
Telling every detail of the problem
In hopes that God would have sympathy
And answer her prayers.
She was praying ever so often.

NOW, HOW WOULD RUTH PRAY

In light of this scripture
If she believed she already had the answer?
She would take the same scriptures
She had been praying and
Thank God she **<u>now</u>** had the answer.

THE FIRST DIFFERENCE SHE NOTICED WAS

There was more peace and joy in her heart.
Then wonders of wonders,
The joyous Presence of God
Filled her heart as she prayed.

SHE ALWAYS WANTED TO ABIDE IN HIS PRESENCE.

Ruth would say to herself, "Today I am going to abide more."
At the end of the day it had not happened.
But now it was happening as she prayed this different way.

BEFORE, SHE WAS PRAYING AS IF SHE HAD

To beg and plead and do something,
As if Jesus never died and gave her
All the promises in the Word
And all the blessings of heaven.

BUT NOW SHE WAS PRAYING FROM

The resurrection side of the cross
As if she already had all these answers
And all she had to do was agree
That the promises were hers.
What a revelation!

ONE MAN SAID,

"I feel like I am lying when I say
I have my answer when I do not have it."

Romans 4:17 God...Calleth those things that be not as though they were.

DO YOU THINK IT IS OK

To follow God's pattern?
God told Israel, "I have given you the land"
When they didn't have it yet.

Psalms 78: 32 "For all this they sinned still, and believed not for His wondrous works. Therefore their days did he consumed in vanity, and their years in trouble"

All God wanted Ruth to do was
Agree with the Word of God,
That the answer was now hers.
It became hers when Jesus died on the cross.

WE RECEIVE OUR ANSWERS TO PRAYER

Just like we receive our salvation—by faith and confession.

Romans 10: 9-10 If thou shalt confess with thy mouth the Lord Jesus, and believe in thine heart that God hath raised him from the dead, thou shalt be saved. For with the heart, man believeth unto righteousness: and with the mouth confession is made unto salvation.

WE KNEW IT WAS IMPORTANT TO BELIEVE.

So in the past if Ruth had a problem
She would try to work up
A feeling of believing,
But most times, that feeling was just not there.

WHEN SHE MADE HER PRAYER BOOKS,

She realized they were all scriptures.
She believed when Jesus died,
All the promises of God became hers.

2 Corth. 1:20 For all the promises of God in him are yea, and in him amen, unto the Glory of God by us.

And all the blessings of heaven became hers
So the believing part was already done.

WHAT WAS THERE LEFT TO DO?

Speak it with her mouth.
"You mean that is all there is to it?"

IT BOILS DOWN TO THIS…

She agrees with the Word of God
That what the Word says is now hers.
God's ways are so simple
That even a child can do them.

RUTH FOUND FIVE SCRIPTURES

She was to do all the time:
Psalms 1:2 In His law doth he mediate day and night;
John 15:4 Abide in Me and I in you;
1 Thessalonians 5:16 Rejoice evermore;
1 Thessalonians 5: 17 Pray without ceasing; and,
1 Thessalonians 5: 18 In everything give thanks.

RUTH TOLD THE LORD,

"Those are five different things.
How can I do five different things
At one time? That is impossible."

WHEN SHE PUT HER PRAYER BOOK TOGETHER

The Lord said, "All five are in
Your Prayer Strategy Resource Book.
It is like a combination lock
That opens the resources of heaven into her situations.

SHE IS MEDITATING ON THE WORD OF GOD

As she prays, thinking what is it like
Now that she has the answer.
As she meditates, the Lord opens her understanding
To many scriptural insights.

HER MIND IS ON LOVING GOD

For all He has done and what Ruth sees is hers.
And that brings His loving, joyous
Presence into her heart. She is then abiding.

SHE REJOICES THAT ALL THESE PROMISES

Are now hers. The continuous
Rejoicing is building faith in her.
She can be thankful in the midst of all situations.

Romans 8:28 ...All things work together for good for those who love the Lord.

RUTH'S GOAL IS TO PRAY WITHOUT CEASING.

It includes all these scriptures:
Meditating on the Word; practicing His presence;
Rejoicing no matter what is happening; and
Being thankful that God is working good
Even in negative situations.

THIS IS LIKE A COMBINATION LOCK

That activates the word of God.
(Jesus is the Word of God)
God brings forth His pleasure and plan
He has been waiting to give to her and others.

THIS WAY OF PRAYER

Activated a ministry for Ruth.
From praying the "Go-Ye" page
When she was 65 years old,
God sent her all over the world
With this good news of great joy.

MONEY CAME IN FOR RUTH TO

Publish books, set up an office,
Pay for her travels --
All from praying the "Prosper" page.

THIRD STRATEGY: AGREEING IN PRAYER

MANY PRAYER GROUPS CAME TOGETHER

To pray and all were praying different ways.
Now we find all agreeing on the same prayer
And praying only that
Brought many more answers to prayer.

Matt 18:19 Again I say unto you, that if two of you shall agree on earth as touching anything that they shall ask, it shall be done for them of my Father which is in heaven.

PRAYER GROUP IN SOUTH BEND, IN

People called in prayer requests.
The group met every week
And decided what to pray.
They all prayed the same way all week.

RUTH SHARED PRAYER STRATEGY WITH THEM

Then they chose a prayer
From Prayer Strategy Resource Book.
All would pray the same scriptural prayer all week.
They had so many more answers to prayer.

THEIR FAMILIES PRAYED FROM PRAYER STRATEGY REOURCE BOOK

Family problem? Called each one in the family,
Told page and prayer number from book.
All prayed the same thing.
They found they did not want
To tell a negative report.

FOR WHEN THEY TOLD THE NEGATIVE DETAILS,

Then everyone agreed with the problem,
That the negative was the truth
And they canceled out the answer.
They had agreed to both a negative and a positive.

"A double minded man receives nothing from the Lord."

KENYA, AFRICA

Christian mayor whose political party
Was split because she used city funds
For projects for the city and not for bribes.
There was much anger against her; daily in the newspaper.

RUTH HAD WOMEN'S MEETING IN KENYA

Ruth had prayer book for family.
First page was "Bringing Unity" page.
Ruth said to pray daily for unity
To come to the political party and also to their families.

WOMEN'S GROUP PRAYED "BRINGING UNITY".

In two days, the opposition came to a meeting
At the mayor's house. They were happy and not angry.
God had broken down the middle wall of enmity
And had brought peace.
Now they were one party again.

BEFORE WE LEFT KENYA,

Women were coming to the pastor
Telling how their homes were
Being changed by praying
The "Bringing Unity" page.

FIVE PEOPLE IN A CHURCH IN ILLINOIS:

One after another had cancer.
They put "Healing" page scriptures in the church bulletin.
One after another,
God started a healing process.

WHOLE FAMILY PRAYED

"Bringing Unity" page for daughter who
Did not want to talk to rest of family.
She had closed herself off in her bedroom.
Now she is back to her friendly self.

WILL HUMBLE THEMSELVES AND PRAY

REVIVAL SEED # 2

RECAP: PRAYERS THAT WORK

1. RUTH STAYED HOME

a. Prayed much.
b. Read the Bible through each year.
c. Read books on prayer.
d. Failed in getting result to deepest needs.

2. FIRST PRAYER STRATEGY

a. Went to a church where they taught her to remind God of His promises often.
b. Don't say the negatives.
c. Notebook with titles of needs.
d. Find scripture promises to fit the problem.
e. God answers the deepest heart cry.

3. SECOND PRAYER STRATEGY

a. Getting answers more quickly
b. Praying as if when Jesus died, all the promises of God became hers, all Heaven's blessings hers.
c. Paraphrasing the scripture: "I now have...."
d. God's presence came in, rejoicing in prayer.

4. THIRD PRAYER STRATEGY

a. Groups praying the same prayer
b. From Prayer Strategy Resource Book – now more answers.

5. RESULTS?

a. Worldwide Ministry activated by "Go-Ye" page.
b. Books published, paid for from "Prosper" page.
c. Many people rejoice over their answers to prayer.

Summary: Praying God's Word, paraphrasing the scripture to believed the promise in now mine, no begging, crying, or pleading, but rejoicing. Now God activates His Word according to my needs and the needs of others.

And
Seek
My
Face

FOCUS IN PRAYER

LEARNING FOCUS IN PRAYER:

Perhaps early 70's, Ruth had physical problem, was bedfast.
One day Ruth thought she was going to die.
She didn't think she was worse,
But she had fears and asked Les to bring her hymn books.

AS SHE LAY IN BED,

She looked at the ceiling
Imagining she was looking into Jesus' eyes.
She was extremely focused, singing praises with all her heart.

WHEN SHE WOULD QUIT HER FOCUS,

The fear would come back
But with extreme focus and praise, she was at peace.

Isaiah 26:3 NKJV You will keep him in perfect peace, whose mind is stayed on You, because he trusts in you.

AFTER 4 OR 5 HOURS OF THIS,

Suddenly she heard Les shouting praises to God,
Coming into the bedroom leaping for joy.

THE PRESENCE OF GOD

Had filled their home. The battle was over; all was well.

THEN RUTH HAD A VISION.

It was like the heavens opened and she saw an entity
Working very hard and fast.
She knew it was on behalf of Ruth's concerns.

NEXT DAY THE LORD SAID TO HER,

"I want you to pray this way all the time,"
But Ruth could not do it until….

TWO WEEKS BEFORE 2008 ELECTION

Ruth's new book How To Get a Mate and Keep 'Em
Went to press.
Ruth was so concerned
About the election,
She decided to spend those two weeks
In extreme focus worshiping, loving Jesus.

WITH HER FOCUS ON LOVING AND PRAISING GOD

Something broke loose in Ruth —
The ability to do this often within His joyous presence.

MANY SAY THEY FEEL PRESSURES

In their lives more than any time before,
So when Ruth feels these pressures or burdens,
She switches over to extreme focus, loving God.
It brings peace to her about the situation.

SHE USES THE BURDEN AS A REMINDER

To praise and worship with extreme focus
Her heart filled with God's presence.

<u>Psalms 34:9 The Message</u> **Worship God if you want the best; worship opens the door to His goodness.**
<u>Psalms 31:19 The Message</u> **What a stack of blessings You have piled up for those who worship You.**

VANCOUVER, BC CHURCH FINDS PRAISE SECRET.

Speaker was having a meeting. It wasn't going well.
Lord gave scripture: <u>**Psalms 22:3**</u> **"But thou art holy, thou that inhabitest the praises of Israel"**
Speaker praises the Lord all day.

DURING THE FIRST HYMN OF EVENING SERVICE,

A man got saved while singing the hymn.
The speaker discovered the power of praise.
The speaker continued this and saw a move of God.
He started a church.

HE HAD HIS PEOPLE COME TO CHURCH

An hour ahead of service, spending time praising God,
In the spirit with extreme focus on loving Jesus.

THEY SAW THE CHURCH GROW,

Bondages broken. Family members became missionaries.

<u>**Psalms 149:6-9**</u> **Let the high praises of God be in their mouths, and a two-edged sward be in their hands (sword is the Word of God) to execute vengeance on the nations and punishment on the peoples; To bind their kings with chains and their nobles with fetters of iron; to execute on them the written judgment – This honor have all the saints.**

Psalms 144:1-2 Blessed be the Lord my strength which teacheth my hands to war and my fingers to fight: My goodness, and my fortress; my high tower, and my deliverer; my shield, and he in whom I trust, who subdueth the people under me.

HOW DO WE FIGHT?

When you have done all, "Stand"
With your face before the Lord,
Gazing upon Him, rejoicing!

THE WORD OF GOD IN YOUR MOUTH,

Proclaiming and announcing your victory,
Keeping your focus on Him,
Bringing every thought captive
To line up with His Word.

THE BATTLE?

Not looking at the enemy,
The evil around you or your lack,
But always seeking His face with a heart of love.

2 Corth: 10:4-5 (For the weapons of our warfare are not carnal, but mighty through God to the pulling down of strongholds): casting down imaginations and every high thing that exalted itself against the knowledge of God, and bringing into captivity every thought to the obedience of Christ.

WHEN KING DAVID WAS IN DEEP TROUBLE,

He would keep his face ever before the Lord.
In the scripture we see that
He would soon be praising the Lord.

THE WORST OF DAYS

And the best of days
Ahead for our country?
Yes, judgment has already started
Just as predicted in the Bible
Before the return of Jesus.

BUT ON THE OTHER HAND

We will see many Christians out in the harvest field
For many a suffering one will seek comfort in Christ.

SOME YEARS AGO,

As I was at church praying,
The Lord said, "I have an army.
They are already trained.
I am going to send them out
To the nooks and crannies
To a people just right for their message."

THERE IS A MINISTRY AHEAD

For the type of people who Jesus picked —
The everyday, no-nothings and never have-beens.
They shall be the "sent out" ones, rejoicing as they go.

AS WE SEEK HIS FACE

In these difficult days ahead,
Drawing close to Him,
We will see many miracles.

WE NEED NOT FEAR,

For we will see faith arise in our hearts
To believe for our needs as we put our trust in God.

GOD WILL LEAD US

In ways we have never known before.
What an adventure
As we share our testimonies
Of what God has done for us!

MANY SAY ABOUT THIS TIME AHEAD,

Seek to hear God's voice
For He will encourage you
And tell you what to do.

Psalms 37:18-19, 25-26 The Lord knowest the days of the upright: and their inheritance shall be forever. They shall not be ashamed in the evil time: and in the days of famine they shall be satisfied. I have been young, and now I am old; I have not seen the righteous forsaken, nor his seed begging bread. He is ever merciful and lendeth; and his seed shall be blessed.

Isaiah 26:9 With my soul have I desired thee in the night; yea with my spirit within me will I seek thee early: for when thy judgments are upon the earth, the inhabitants of the earth will learn righteousness.

HEARING GOD'S VOICE INDIVIDUALLY
Without being flaky and weird.

LES AND RUTH PRAYED
Many hours daily with very few visible answers.

LES: "LETS ASK GOD'S OPINION
About what we should pray."

RUTH HAD A LOT OF SUSPICIONS
About people who heard from God (whackos).
Ruth said, " I do not want to do this."

LES SAID TO RUTH:
"Put your pen on your paper and
Ask God to give a word for a starter.
Write what comes to mind.
See if He will give you more words."

THEY WERE NOT IMPRESSED WITH
What they wrote but later, on rereading them,
They thought it was very good.

THEY KEPT DOING THIS
And they began to see the results
In more answers to prayer,
Praying about their church.

PRAYING GOD'S VISION
Is better than us moaning and groaning
About the problems and people of the church.
God has a higher vision than we do.

THEY WOULD DO THIS AT CHURCH PRAYER.
They were doing a big conference.
They asked God what He thought —
What exciting view God had.
It was bigger than anything they dreamed up.

CONFERENCE CAME AND WENT
They looked at what the Lord
Had told them would happen.
Did it really come to pass? Yes, much to their delight!

RUTH THOUGHT:

"Why not ask God about each family member?"

RUTH'S FAMILY PRAYERS:

Seeing weaknesses and praying about them.
This was before she learned Prayer Strategy.

GOD'S PERSPECTIVE:

Positive, delightful, exciting, loving,
And encouraging about each family member.
Now, more prayer results.

HEARING FROM GOD

Is called prophecy.

TESTING PROPHECY:

Does it line up with the Bible?
Does it encourage, build up?
Does it help you to believe God's goodness?

IS PROPHECY PERFECT?

We know a part of it
But not the whole picture.

1Corth 13:9 For we know in part and prophecy in part.

GOOD TOOL IN THE TOOLBOX

When Ruth was bothered
She would ask God, "What do you think?"

WRITING THE ANSWER

Encouraged her and changed her viewpoint.
It put light on her path and comfort to her soul,

RESTORING HER FAITH

So she could believe for the answer
As she went through the problem
And won the battles with faith.

1 Timothy 1:18 This charge I commit unto thee, son Timothy, according to the prophecies which went before thee, that thou by them mightest war a good warfare; Holding faith, and a good conscience; which some having put away concerning faith have made shipwreck.

HEARING GOD'S VOICE IN A GROUP.

Ruth and Les prayed with people
At the close of the service each week,
Same people, same problems in same detail.
No noticeable answers.

THEN RUTH HELD SEMINARS.

Standing in line after her talks,
She spent many hours of hearing long details
Of peoples' problems.

IDEA: PRAYER GUIDELINES

Were given to each one at the end of the service.
They were divided into groups of three.
More in group if time permitted.

INSTRUCTIONS: DO NOT TELL DETAILS OF PROBLEM

Because everyone will agree that is the truth
And then you will pray about those negative details.
You won't get answers because
You have agreed on the problem
And the answer both and a double-minded man
Receives nothing from the Lord.

ONE AT A TIME, EACH PERSON IN THE GROUP

Would tell a prayer need in a few words,
Then the whole group would
Write what they thought God was saying.

EACH ONE TOOK A TURN,

Told what the Lord said and then prayed that.
Then they went on to the next person,
Repeating the same procedure.

WHEN ALLWERE THROUGH,

Each person gave what they wrote
To the person they wrote it for,
So they could run with the vision.

Proverbs 29:18 Where there is no vision, the people perish.

IT GAVE THEM HOPE.

Each prophecy was different
But each blended with the whole picture.

ONE PASTOR COPIED PRAYER GUIDELINES

So his whole congregation
Could follow them the next Sunday.

CHURCH PRAYER GROUPS

Spend more time telling problems than praying.
With asking God what He thinks,
They are much more productive.

SEMINAR IN SINGAPORE

Families with children
Divided up in family groups.
Each told a concern for their family.
How excited these families were
To see these young children write.
Even children too young to write
Had something the Lord was telling them.

RUTH ENCOURAGES PEOPLE

To do this with their families
When conflict arises.
They are able to receive the prophecy
Better than words from parents or siblings.

WHAT A GOOD TOOL FOR MARRIAGES

To settle conflicts or just to bring encouragement
To their situations.

CHRISTIAN SCHOOL CLASS OUT OF CONTROL,

Teacher was in desperation, had the children write
What God was telling them.

ANSWERS FROM GOD:

You are copying someone's
Spelling paper during spelling test.
Another: You copied someone else's homework.
They were able to receive the words.

THE WHOLE CLIMATE OF THE CLASS CHANGED

As the teacher continued with this practice.
Children said, "Let's share with other classes."
They had the same good results.

REVIVAL SEED # 3

RECAP: SEEK HIS FACE – HEARING HIS VOICE

1. PRAYING WITH FOCUS OF LOVE

a. Face before the Lord in worship.
b. Great power from God is activated.
c. Relieves our burdens.
d. Results of people coming to church early to worship.
e. Extreme focus of love during stressful times.

2. WARFARE PRAYING

a. King David in deep trouble.
b. His face was always before the Lord.
c. Our battle, stand still, face before the Lord rejoicing.
d. Not looking at the enemy, but at the Lord.
e. Then the Lord fights for you.

3. HEARING GOD'S VOICE INDIVIDUALLY

a. His opinion higher than ours.
b. Testing what you hear.
c. Encouraging you to win the battle of faith.
d. An important tool we need at this time.

4. HEARING GOD'S VOICE IN A GROUP

a. Prayer Guidelines.
b. Praying for concerns in a group.
c. Each asking God what He thinks.
d. Sharing the thoughts or writings.
e. Praying about thoughts you get.
f. People encouraged and uplifted about their concerns.
g. Use in family, children, marriages.

Summary: The power of God is released as we have our faces before the Lord in extreme focus of worship during our trials, hearing God's voice to encourage us and build us up in these days ahead for us at this time in our country.

And
Turn
From
Their
Wicked
Ways

SEEKING REVIVAL FOR OURSELVES

RUTH'S HUSBAND LES SOLD BUSINESS,
Came home to pray, fast and study scripture.
Their decision: to seek the Lord for revival.
They read many books on revival.

THEY SETTLED ON TWO BOOKS
Written about the same revival
That was going on in Rwanda, Africa.
Calvary Road by Roy Hession
Continuous Revival by Norman Grubbs.

WHY WAS THIS REVIVAL STILL GOING ON
After many years when most revivals
Last about three years?

NORMAN GRUBBS INVITED RWANDA MEN
To his large mission station in England.
A layman from Rwanda shared
About the revelation of sin in his life.

WHEN HE WAS THROUGH SPEAKING,
A man stood and said, "I see I have the same sin."
The speaker replied, "Gentlemen, this is revival."

THE REVIVAL IN RWANDA CONTINUED
As the laymen held meetings,
They shared about sin revealed
And what repentance meant —
Just turning away from that sin.

LES, RUTH AND THEIR GOOD FRIEND BECKY
Would read from these books each day
To see if revival would happen to them.
They began to notice sin in their lives.
Their world became brighter — a noticeable difference.

THEY PRAYED TOGETHER DAILY.
Soon, they were aware if one of them
Had ought against the other.
They found often their sin originated
In one of them being offended by little things.

ONE DAY THEY GATHERED TO PRAY,
Les said, "Alright, who has sin?"
No one said a word. We waited in silence.

FINALLY BECKY SAID, "I DON'T WANT TO SAY,
Because you will laugh at me."
Les, with much prodding said,
"Come on Becky, tell us what it is."

THE DAY BEFORE WHEN BECKY CAME OVER,
Becky had a red shirt and slacks on.
Les, sitting on the porch said,
"Becky, I see you have your devil suit on."

LES LOVED TO JOKE; BECKY WAS OFFENDED.
Les asked her to forgive him.
Now, all was clear to pray again.

WHAT KIND OF SIN ARE WE TALKING ABOUT?
We found out from the Rwanda books that
Sin was worry, fear, anger, unforgiveness,
Gossip, envy, touchiness, sensitiveness, etc.

SIN IS COVERED UP
By our human nature, feelings, self righteousness.
That's why we do not recognize
These things as sin. "That's just the way I am."

THE RWANDA PEOPLE FOUND
They had to notice what was
Going on in their minds moment by moment
And turn away from their very thoughts
So their sin wouldn't captivate their minds
And take root in their hearts.

ANOTHER BIG HELP WAS ALLOWING OTHERS
To tell each other sin unnoticed by that person.
They welcomed that admonishment,
Wanting to be the best for Jesus' sake.

TIME PASSED AND WE GOT AWAY
From this focus in our lives,
But it was a stepping stone to other insights
That would be developed later.

OTHER BOOKS OF INFLUENCE

BASILEA SCHLINK

Ministered to groups of young girls
Before World War II in Germany.

THE WAR CAME.

She was in demand as a speaker
All over Germany.
People crowded to hear her.

THE LORD TOLD HER

She had lost her "bridal love for Christ"
That she had when she first came to know Him.
How could that be, for this was
The most fruitful time in her life?

SHE ASKED THE LORD

To take her into a deeper repentance
And God answered her prayer.

SOMETIMES HER SIN WOULD SHOW

In embarrassing ways in front of others.
We repent better when our sin
Unveils for all to see.

GOD BROUGHT HER INTO

The joy of the bridal love for Jesus
She had enjoyed when
She first came to know Him.

THE LAST BIG BOMBING

At the end of World War II
Was in Darmstadt, Germany.

IT WAS SO DEVASTATING,

It caused people to seek the Lord,
And a great revival broke out
As God touched people's hearts in the city.

OUT OF THIS REVIVAL

Basilea Schlink started
The Lutheran Sisterhood of Mary
With the young girls she had
Been ministering to.

THE SISTERHOOD OF MARY:
Their dress and way was much like
A Catholic sisterhood convent.
Their devotion was to be only to Jesus.

THE SISTERS WERE GIVEN LAND
To build their Convent on.
They did all the building work themselves.

NEARBY WAS A PRAYER TENT.
Some were in continual prayer for the projects.

IF THINGS DID NOT GO RIGHT,
They would all gather and ask,
"Who has the sin?" God would reveal it
To a sister's heart, she would repent,
Then all would go well again.
They could get back to work.

THEY DID NOT OWN ANYTHING
But sometimes the sin was that
Someone had an item they treasured
More than Jesus.

THEY BELIEVED JESUS SET THEM FREE
From the curse; therefore, they should not
Have bugs in their garden. If they found bugs,
They would ask the Lord where the sin was.

THIS TOOK SOME TIME OF SEARCHING.
They would pick the bugs off by hand,
But the day came when there were
No longer bugs eating their garden.

I SAW SOME OF THEM IN PERSON
At the Catholic Renewal
In the 1970's at Notre Dame.
These sisters were like tinkling bells of joy.

THEY HAD LET GOD PRUNE
Their hearts in such a way
That they had continuous revival
They lived to please the one they loved the most,
Even to the smallest matters of the heart.

THE LOST PAGE

NOW YEARS LATER

I thought about those days of repenting.
I decide to pray the "Lost" page in the
Prayer Strategy Resource Book
To see if God would dredge out of my heart
Some more sin "unnoticed".

CINCINNATI "BE IN HEALTH SEMINARS"

Now named Restoring Life International
Called to have me speak.
They found my Prayer Strategy Resource Book
And thought it would be a good resource book
For their people to use after seminars.

WHEN I LEFT THEY GAVE ME

A big white book A More Excellent Way, Be In Health
by Henry Wright.
I thought, "I don't have time to read this."
I gave it to my daughter. "Mom, you need to read this."

HENRY WRIGHT WOULD PRAY FOR PEOPLE

To get healed, but he saw no healings.
"Lord, I want to know why people are not healed," he said.

GOD BEGAN TO SHOW INSIGHTS IN THE BIBLE,

Attitudes and sins that opened the door
For particular diseases to come in.
When people found the root cause and
Repented (turned away from), many were healed.
Again, there had been sin unnoticed.

OUR FAMILY MEMBERS ATTENDED HIS SEMINAR

In Thomaston, GA for a week.
Checking in, we wrote down our physical problems.
At the end of the week, they prayed for us,
Having written what they thought
Might be the root cause of our diseases.

A WHOLE NEW VIEWPOINT SURFACED

About my past, sinful attitudes;
Thoughts about my growing-up years were completely
changed. Now, no pain in my body.

ONE AREA OF SIN WAS

Not liking ourselves, looking in the mirror, "Ugh!"
When God made us, He said, "This is good."
Our bodies react to negative thoughts and words,
Opening the door for the curse of sickness to come in.

ONE WOMAN'S REVIVAL MARRIAGE

First fifteen years were wonderfully happy.
Husband loved Wife unconditionally.

WHAT WAS THIS MARRIAGE LIKE?

They were likeminded the way they raised the children,
They were each other's best friend.
They were of one mind -- in harmony.
"And the two shall become one."
They had revival in their marriage.

WIFE READ BOOKS ABOUT CHRISTIAN HOME.

She saw areas where Husband should change.
She tried to encourage him to change. He did not change.

THEN SIN CAME IN.

When Husband did not change to suit Wife,
Resentment (sin) and bitterness (sin) hid in her heart.
Wife did not respect (sin) him as before.
But it was sin unnoticed by Wife
Because "She was right in her own eyes".

RESULT:

The oneness of mind was gone.
"Lord, what happened that the oneness is not as before?"
She begged often to know that answer.
Husband was not quite the spiritual leader as before.

RESULT:

Wife developed arthritis, pain, needed knee replacements.
They still had a great marriage,
Loved each other, prayed together, enjoyed each other,
But the oneness of revival was not there as before.

AT THIS TIME

That resentment never surfaced,
Was not recognized as sin. It stayed hidden.
Wife would not know until years later.

SIN REVEALED LEADS TO REVIVAL.

Les passed away and Ruth married Dan.
After one year, three things bothered Ruth about Dan.
Oh no, she did not want to be bothered.
She knew better
Than trying to change a husband.

SEMINAR CHURCH OF GOD CAMPMEETING

Ruth spoke at seminar and told them what to do.
"Don't let the dark thoughts in,
And bless them often."

"I WILL DO WHAT I PREACH."

She practiced. No dark thoughts and blessed him often.
Third day, walking through the house,
The Spirit of God filled the house.
Dan came in the room. "Dan, do you feel that?"
"Yes." She told him about the three things.

DAN: "WHAT WERE THE THREE THINGS?"

Ruth said, "I don't know.
The Lord took them out of my mind."

RUTH HAD HEARD THAT GOD

Was going to give an "Open Heaven".
She wondered what that would be like.
She thought, "I think, this is an Open Heaven."

"LORD, YOU MEAN THE ONLY THING

That stops me from having revival in my home
Are my negative thoughts?
I can have an Open Heaven all the time?
I am going after that."

WHAT IS THIS REVIVAL LIKE?

It is not my love,
But God's love that flows over us.
Sometimes singly, but most times on both of us.
We are amazed and talk about it daily.

NO CHALLENGES?

Of course, in life there will always be challenges.
There are times when "I want my way".
It is a moment-by-moment decision.

YOU MAY SUFFER, LICK YOUR WOUNDS

"Not fair! My way is better."
But what Ruth wanted most is this revival.
God's presence is worth far more
Than Ruth having to have her way.

HOW DOES RUTH TREAT HER HUSBAND?

She honors him, respects him, esteems him,
And serves him as head of the home.
The more she does this, the more she sees
The great person she is married to.

A WOMAN CAN BUILD UP

Or tear down her own home.
When she finds her place in God's order
As a wife and becomes like Jesus,
He humbling himself and taking second place,
Suffering for us so we can be free,
So then Ruth can have Heaven's Revival in her home.

LOOK AT THE PICTURE ON THE COVER.

There is a cross for everyone and there's a cross for me.
Jesus on the cross released revival for us.

THE ONLY THING THAT IS SUFFERING

Is your natural self, the self we are all born with.

RUTH PUBLISHED

How to Get a Mate and Keep 'Em.
Later, the thought came to her mind,
"I think the seeds to revival are in
The 'Keep'em part of the book."

SHE TOOK EXCERPTS FROM SOME OF THE PAGES

To show how we are the key
To the answers of our concerns.
Where *we* change, we will see
The atmosphere around us change also.

WE COULD SEE REVIVAL NOT ONLY IN THE HOME

But a pattern for revival for our churches, city, and country.
It begins with God's people.
"If my people who are called by my name…."
It starts with us.

Excerpts from: <u>HOW TO GET A MATE AND KEEP'EM</u>

WOMEN KEY TO THE ANSWER

In restoration of the home, marriages, and children,
Like a mighty army, for the following reasons.
The same concepts can be used for men and even children.

WOMEN ARE THE HEART OF THE HOME Page 62-63

God made them to love,
Care about their family.
They want things right.

WHEN THINGS ARE NOT RIGHT,

Women tend to attack the problem,
Their husbands and their children,
All because they are hurting,
Wanting to solve the problem
With those they love.
This leads to the road of destruction,
The tearing down of the home.

Proverbs 14:1 the Book A wise woman builds her house, while a foolish woman tears hers down by her own effort.
When I would read the above scripture, I used to wonder how am I tearing down, and how am I raising up my home? I did not have a clue.

"I AM GOING TO HAVE MY WAY."

One woman said,
"I will keep at him until he changes.
I know how to get my way."

THE WOMAN IS "RIGHT".

She becomes angry, hurting,
Suffering. "No one cares."
Has unforgiveness, bitterness.
"I AM RIGHT!! NO FAIR!!

THE GREAT THING ABOUT WOMEN,

When they find a way for
Things to change, they will do it
Because they care sooooo much
For their families.

WOMEN, QUIT RAILING ON THEM.

Keep your mouth shut.
Give up your anger
Even though you are right.

WORK AT SWITCHING

What goes on in your mind
From the negative situation
To the positives of your answer.
Not easy, but make yourself do it.

FIND PRAYERS THAT FIT THE SITUATION

In Prayer Strategy Resource Book
Get into a quiet place.
Make it a priority to spend time
Soaking in the answer. Do it often.
Let the word of God
Do the work for you.

PRAY THE "FORGIVING AND BLESSING" PAGE

In the Prayer Strategy Resource Book.
Pray it often until that word
Works forgiveness in your heart.

BLESS THEM OFTEN,

Every time the negative creeps in.
There is so much power in blessing.
When God hears you bless
Then He comes down to bless the situation.

ELDER'S WIFE CAME TO VISIT.

She told us how bad her husband was.
She wanted a divorce.

LES SAID: "BLESS AND CURSE NOT."

Lady: "What do you mean?"
Les: "Bless and curse not."
Lady: "Oh, I get it!" and she left.

SEVERAL MONTHS LATER:

Ruth said: "How is your marriage?"
Lady: "Great! I realized I was cursing him.
I started to bless him. Now we are happy."

HOW TO GET A MATE AND KEEP'EM Page 29

WHEN PRAYING FOR TROUBLED FAMILIES

The offending one gets better
But they still get a divorce. We wonder: Why?

THE OFFENDED ONE HAS NOT FORGIVEN

"Isn't your mate doing better?"
"Yes, but not enough."

WHEN WE DON'T FORGIVE,

God turns us over to the tormentors.
The offender may be wrong, you may be right,
But if you don't forgive,
You also become the sinner.

YOUR TORMENT COMING FROM GOD?

Mathew 18:22-35 How often do we forgive "seven times?" Until seventy times seven Jesus said. Story of the servant who did not pay the King what he owed and was being put in jail, but was forgiven and set free of a big debt. Then this servant went to fellow servant who owed him a little and put him in prison. The King found out. 34. And the Lord was wroth and delivered him to the tormentors, till he should pay all that was due unto him. 35 Jesus said "So likewise shall My heavenly Father do also to you, if ye from your hearts forgive not everyone his brother their trespasses

WHY THE DIVORCE?

Even though the offender is doing better,
The offended one is now being tormented
By our Heavenly Father Himself,
Because she cannot forgive from the heart
And can find no peace in her situation.

GOD'S ORDER Page 35 "How To Get a Mate and Keep'em"

BIBLE CHAIN OF COMMAND

God first,
Husband next,
Then the wife,
Then the children.

TRUST IN GOD

Not in man.
God has everything in control.

WHAT IF HUSBAND'S WAY FAILS?

He just might fail.
God will still work good
In and through the situation.
Again, Trust in God.

SHOWING HUSBAND RESPECT

Page 43 "How To Get a Mate and Keep'em"

I respect and reverence my husband. I notice him, regard him, honor him, prefer him, venerate him, esteem him; and I defer to him, praise him; and love him and admire him exceedingly. Ephes. 5:33b AMP Let the wife see that she respects and reverences her husband-that she notices him, regards him, honors him, prefers him, venerates and esteems him; and that she defers to him, praises him, and loves and admires him exceedingly. Page 69 # 14. Prayer Strategy Resource Book

RUTH PREFERS HIM

More than relatives, more than her best friends,
More than her children. He is number one.

RUTH DEFERS TO HIM.

That means she does what he wants.
She tries to do what pleases him.

RUTH PRAYS THE SCRIPTURE OFTEN

Because her human nature
Wants to run the show.
Does not always want to defer to him.

WHEN RUTH MISSES THE MARK

She repents.

BY THE POWER OF THAT WORD,

God is changing Ruth to do what the Word says.

RESULT?

God's blessing is on her marriage.

CARING FOR THE UNLOVING

Excerpts from How To Get A Mate and Keep'em Page 34-35

RUTH: CARING FOR OLDER LADY

She was hard to get along with;
Picky and demanding about everything,
But she had no one else.
Who would put up with her demands?

EASY? NO!

Ruth took upon herself the role of a servant;
Became obedient to her wishes
Because she needed Ruth's help.

CHRISTIANITY IS NOT FOR WIMPS.

Let this mind be in you
Which was in Christ Jesus:
He took upon himself
The form of a servant.

I DO NOT LIKE BEING A DOORMAT.

Was Jesus a doormat or not?
He became a doormat for us.
Thus opened a door to heaven's blessings
And earthly joys for us.

WE ARE ALSO CALLED INTO THIS MINISTRY.

When you find out what
Your true ministry is —
That when you serve others,
You are serving Him.

HOW DID I ACT IN THIS MINISTRY?

I did not answer back
Nor tell her off
Nor make demands (for that never did any good).

WAS IT ALWAYS PLEASANT? NO.

Was I defeated? No.
We had a happy relationship.

1 Corinthians 1:18. For the preaching of the cross is to them that perish foolishness, but unto us which are saved it is the power of God.

WHAT IS LOVE? Page 47 How to Get a Mate and Keep'em
I now know more and have greater discernment on how to have my love abound toward others. Instead of looking at the bad, I am now able to approve what is excellent, so I am sincere and without offense until the day of Christ. I am filled with the good fruits of righteousness that you have given me, Christ, which is all to your glory. Page 29 Prayer Strategy Resource Book & Page 47 'Get a Mate and Keep'em'

BY-PRODUCTS OF LOOKING AT THE GOOD

You will not an offence to God.
You will understand how to love others.
You will be filled with fruit of righteousness:
Love, joy, peace, longsuffering, gentleness
Goodness, faith, meekness, temperance.

WHEN WE LOOK AT OTHERS' FAULTS,

We bind them and they cannot get free.
Our prayers for them do not work.

BY LOOKING AT THE GOOD IN OTHERS,

We set them free; we become like God whose love
Sees only our good.

FINISHING THE WORK OF CHRIST

How do we do that?

THE WAY OF THE CROSS

We give up our hurt and pain.
Choose not to hold onto the negatives about others.
Be servants to those who don't deserve it.
We will forgive them. We will bless them.
We will pray for them. Do good to them.

THIS WILL SET THEM FREE.

Just as Jesus set us free, He suffered, was beaten,
Giving up everything for us.

WHEN WE FOLLOW THIS WAY

Then God comes, others are set free,
Revival – the joy of His presence.
Great is our reward, not only in heaven,
But here on earth.

LADY WHO WAS THE KEY TO HER ANSWER

THE "NO HOPE PEOPLE"

Suffering with their situation
Are those who, when they find how to pray,
Will give time and effort to pray,
Giving up other things
Because they are desperate for answers.

ONE SUCH WOMAN PHONED RUTH.

She just got out of the hospital.
Her husband had beaten her, broken her arm.
She knew she couldn't live that way
With her life in danger.

"BUT I STILL LOVE HIM,

I don't want to leave him.
Is there something I can do
To change my situation?"

RUTH ANSWERED, "TRY THIS:

I know this isn't true all the time,
For some spouses are mentally sick,
But so far I have not met an abused wife
Who didn't have an abusive tongue."

RUTH KNEW SHE WAS A LITTLE "SPIT-FIRE".

Ruth told her, "When he talks angry,
Don't answer back. Hold your fire!

BE NICE TO HIM, PLEASANT.

Cook what he wants.
What are his favorite foods?
Is there something he wants you to do?
Then do it."

HE WAS AN ALCOHOLIC

Get home at 2:00 AM drunk
After being with his girlfriend.

HE GOT PICKED UP FOR DRUNKEN DRIVING

Coming through suburb of the city.
Police said that if they caught him coming
Through their city drunk after dark again,
They would put him in jail.

HE WAS AFRAID OF GOING TO JAIL

So he began coming home before dark.
After many months of him
Sleeping on the davenport,
She called to tell me one day she was happy!
"He slept in my bed last night."

SHE BAKED HIS FAVORITE PIE.

His reply, "Why are you doing this?"

FOR THE FIRST TIME IN TWO YEARS

He took her and the four children
Someplace in the car.
They went to the drive-in for supper.

YES, SHE HAD SOME DOWNERS.

Sometimes she would call crying and upset.
But then she would regroup,
Get encouraged and work at her situation.
Things would mellow out again.

HE HAD FLOWERS DELIVERED TO HER DOOR

On their wedding anniversary.
Never had that happened before.

HE BECAME FRIENDS WITH A CHRISTIAN AT WORK,

He quit drinking so much.
Last time I heard from them,
They were moving out of town
Next door to the Christian.

WHO CHANGED FIRST?

She did.
The one who is hurting
Is the one who changes first.

CHILDREN CHANGING

From Ruth and Les' Sunday School class:
An eight year old girl
Whose older brother
Teased her all the time.

SHE WAS COMPLAINING ON SUNDAY MORNINGS.

Finally Les said, "You're the one who starts the fight."
Her reply, "No! No! He's the one who starts it."
Les: "There wouldn't be a fight if you didn't answer back.
Don't answer back when he teases you."

WHEN THE BROTHER

Didn't get a rise out of his sister
And couldn't get her upset anymore,
It was no fun for him
So he quit teasing her.

THE MOTHER REPORTED TO LES AND RUTH,

"Our home is so peaceful.
I am so grateful."

ANOTHER CHILDREN'S STORY

From Les and Ruth's Sunday School class:
A crying eight-year-old who lived with her Grandma said,
"My Grandma and I are not getting along. We argue."

LES SAID, "ASK YOUR GRANDMA WHAT YOU

Can do to make her happy and do it."
Next Sunday: " I asked my Grandma
And she told me what she wanted me to do.
I did it and now we are happy."

RUTH SAID TO THE OTHER CHILDREN,

"Why don't you go home and ask
Your parents if there is something
You can do to make them happy."

THE CHILDREN SQUIRMED IN THEIR SEATS,

Looking down, and we could tell
They did not want to do this.

BUT ABOUT EACH SUNDAY AFTER THAT,
At least one child would say
They had done that and they reported
Favorable results.

PARENTS CAME AND TOLD US
The amazing results,
The changes that came to their households
Because their children had changed.
Yes, even children can be missionaries in their own homes.

LESTER SUMMRAL GAVE
Instructions for a good marriage:
Find out what they want and do it.

GOOD WOMEN
Praying the Word of God
For their husbands,
Having the joy of seeing them change.
Husbands being anointed by God to serve.

UNHAPPINESS IN FAMILIES CAUSED BY
Concentrating on other's faults,
Using arguments and persuasion to try to change them.
The negative thoughts produce a negative future,
Destroying homes and lives.

THE ONLY WAY TO HELP OR HEAL ANYONE:
Forgive; don't look at the sin or sickness.
Choose to let go of it
Knowing that God is doing a good work in them.

WHEN WOMEN RECOGNIZE THIS TRUTH
And get quietly before the Lord,
They will see a change in their men
Through the Lord working through them.

THINK OF ALL THE MEN AND CHILDREN
Who will be set free to serve the Lord
Because women have the key
To know how to make this happen.

RHONDA'S STORY

Life crashed around her, losing her baby boy
In an ugly divorce, day-by-day despair.

SOUGHT THE LORD

Through TV programs.
Now knows the Lord Jesus Christ.

FOUND <u>PRAYER STRATEGY RESOURCE BOOK</u>

The Word of God was activated into her life
Through this way of prayer.
Her anger and pain were relieved. She was able to forgive.

IN <u>HOW TO GET A MATE AND KEEP'EM</u>

She found that she is the key
To the answers for her second marriage.
She gave up being the boss.
She is learning to respect and honor her husband.

GOD'S RESPONSE?

His blessing becomes
Stronger and stronger in her marriage
As she practices these concepts.
She finds that where she changes,
The environment around her changes.

NOW SHE IS FILLED

With the desire to share
Her good news of great joy with others.

WHO IS SHE FINDING?

Other people who are suffering
With great pain and losses,
Their lives also crashing around them.

THESE PEOPLE WHO PERHAPS NEVER

Wanted God in their lives before.
They thought they did not need a Savior.
They are now ready to hear her story.

HOPE IS SEEPING INTO THEIR HEARTS.

As they see how they, too,
Can have this new power
Working for them and their needs.

RUTH WONDERED MANY TIMES,

"What were the early Christians like?"
Now she knows. They were like Rhonda,
Ordinary people, filled with a zeal
To share their good news with others.

WHEN THEY TOLD THEIR STORIES,

Others believed Jesus was for them also,
That He wanted to meet their needs.
They then put their trust in Him
And their lives were changed.

THEN THEY HAD A STORY TO TELL.

This was God's multiplication program.
No college degree in Theology,
But just testimonies from ordinary people,
The kind of people Jesus hung out with.

You have given me a new song to sing of praise unto You, my God. Now many hear the glorious things You have done for me, and stand in awe before You and put their trust in You. Psalms 40:3 TLB He has given me a new song to sing of praises to our God. Now many will hear the glorious things he did for me, and stand in awe before the Lord, and put their trust in him. From Prayer Strategy Resource Book page 6 # 7

THE LORD IS SPEAKING TO MANY

That in these days and in the days ahead,
As our economy collapses more and more,
Instead of our government saying, "I will give you…."
People are finding they are left with nothing.

THEN IT WILL BE THE ORDINARY PEOPLE

Just like in the New Testament
Who will draw along side
And share the Gospel with these hurting people.
They will find that God will be their provider.

WE WILL SEE A MIGHTY MOVE OF GOD

That could never have happened
In any other way —
God turning bad situations
Into testimonies and more testimonies.

AND TURN FROM THEIR WICKED WAYS

REVIVAL SEED # 4

RECAP: RECOGNIZING SIN AND TURNING AWAY

1. SEEKING REVIVAL

a. Finding sin is hidden within our human nature.
b. Learning to recognize when it comes to the surface.
c. It is the little things that bother us.
d. Things like worry, fear, anger, unforgiveness, gossip, envy, touchiness, etc.
e. Les and Ruth read daily about this and saw a difference.

2. REVIVAL MARRIAGE

a. Ruth married Dan; three things about him bothered her.
b. At seminar she taught, don't think on negative and bless.
c. Third day of keeping negatives out and blessing Dan, the presence of God filled her home.
d. Ruth: "If I keep negatives out can I have God's presence all the time?"
e. Yes, it has happened. Revival!!!!

3. THE HURTING ONE IS KEY TO THE ANSWER

a. How you can change so the atmosphere changes.
b. The power of blessing and cursing not.

4. HAVING THE MIND OF CHRIST JESUS

a. Giving up your rights.
b. Taking second place.
c. Becoming a servant.
d. Is that easy? Giving up your feelings? No!
e. Especially when you are right.
f. The way of the cross.
g. That is where the power of God comes in the situation.

Summary: Sin unnoticed is hidden in the inner person, blocking the blessings God wants to give us. This segment tells how you can change in a way that God can now heal your situation. You are the key to the answer. You are the key to REVIVAL.

"Then
Will I
Hear
From
Heaven"
In Our
Churches

REVIVAL IN MY CHURCH?

PEOPLE SAY, "IF I ONLY KNEW A GOOD CHURCH,

I would go to it."
Those who say that could be the "key to their answer".

AS WE HAVE LEARNED ALREADY,

The one who is hurting
Is often the one who is the key to the answer.
They are the ones who will pray
Because they want to be free of their hurts.

REVIVAL IS ALREADY OURS AS CHRISTIANS.

When Jesus suffered and died on the cross,
That revival was made available to us.
It is already ours.

THE CHURCH IS MADE UP OF CHRISTIANS.

If we are not experiencing revival,
Then there is sin in the church unnoticed.

WE HAVE ALREADY RESEARCHED

Just where we can change to
Bring revival into the home.
The same principles apply to the church.

Thank You, Lord, that I have chosen life for myself and my children by choosing to bless others and not to put a curse on them with bad words and thoughts. Deut. 30:19 NIV I call heaven and earth as witnesses today against you, that I have set before you life and death, blessing and cursing; therefore choose life, that both you and your descendants may live.

WHEN I FIRST READ THIS PRAYER ABOVE,

I was convicted of sin.
I said bad words about people.
I thought if it was the truth, it was OK to say it.

IT IS PLAIN THAT THIS BOOK

Deals with the choice that is before us.
We are the ones to choose life
For ourselves, our children, our church,
And even our country,
Just by what we think and say.

OR WE TEAR DOWN

Our homes and our churches
By what we choose to think or say.

THE PEOPLE IN THE CHURCH

Are the ones who are given the choice —
A church that has Revival
Or a church that dries up and dies.

WHEN WE IN THE CHURCH

Realize we are the problem, we are the sinners,
When we care enough to change, we can have
An open heaven flowing in our church.

WE GO BY OUR HUMAN NATURE,

Our feelings, our hurts, our pains,
What somebody did or said
Or what somebody didn't do or say.

LIVING THE CRUCIFIED LIFE,

Being like Jesus,
Being humble, giving up our rights,
Taking second place,
Blessing instead of cursing others,
This is, not easy, it is the way of the cross.

THEN GOD WILL COME IN

And will bless us His way
And by His goodness.

OUR HUMAN NATURE IS ALWAYS WITH US.

Moment-by-moment, we will be looking
To make this great sacrifice
Of dying to self and taking up our cross,
Which will release an open heaven to us and our church.

WHEN THE NEGATIVES COME INTO OUR HEARTS,

That is unforgivenes.
When we don't forgive
Because we feel we are right,
Then God himself sends a tormenting spirit,
Oppression on us, just too hard to stay in that church.
We can hardly stand it.

ANOTHER BLOCKAGE.

There is an order of authority
In the church
Just like in the home.

AUTHORITY IN THE CHURCH:

God first,
Pastor next,
Then the people.

WHEN PEOPLE LINE UP

With the proper attitude
Toward their Pastor,
Recognizing his authority,
Then God blesses.
Give honor to whom honor is due.

STEP DOWN,

Humble yourself
And let him be the leader,
Trusting God for the answers.

WHEN MY HUSBAND DAN

Was a soldier fighting in World War II,
The soldiers said, “Yes Sir”
To their officers.

WERE OFFICERS ALWAYS RIGHT?

No. Dan said the war would
Have been over much sooner
But some of the decisions of top officers
Were mistakes.

WHAT DID THE LOWER RANKING OFFICERS SAY?

“Yes Sir.”
God honors the chain of command.

DAVID COULD HAVE KILLED SAUL

While Saul was looking to kill him
Because Saul was jealous.
But David would not do that to God’s
Appointed one who had authority over him.

WHEN WE FOLLOW AUTHORITY,
Whether in the home, our church, or our country,
We have to trust in God for results.

IN MY TOWN
Some said, "When five of the bullies
Of that church pass away,
Then that church will grow."

WHEN BULLIES ARE OUT
Of God's chain of command
And "hog tie" the Pastor.
What can the people do?

BLESS THEM AT EVERY THOUGHT,
Pray the Word of God for them.
Keep the negatives out of your mind
And you will see God work to set them free.

WOULD IF YOU HAVE A PASTOR
Who is a problem?
The same goes for the Pastor.

WE CAN PRAY THE "PASTOR" PAGE
From Prayer Strategy Resource Book.
Put the positives in your mouth
Instead of the negatives in your mouth and heart.
He will be blessed.

PASTOR: 10 INTERCESSORS PRAY "PASTOR" PAGE.
Pastor said he got creative thoughts.
His preaching became more inspired.
The church grew, doubled in size.

CHURCHES PRAYED "BRINGING UNITY" PAGE.
People were more friendly and loving.
They wanted to stay around after church to visit.

ONE CHURCH PUTS "PROSPER" PAGE
On overhead every Sunday.
One person prays the scripture,
The congregation all say the prayers together.
Now they have money to meet their needs.

REVIVAL SEED # 5

RECAP: YOU BRINGING CHURCH REVIVAL?

IF I ONLY KNEW A GOOD CHURCH........

a. Jesus already won revival for us.
b. Why we do not have it in the church?
c. People in the pew are the reason.

HOW WE TEAR DOWN OUR CHURCH

a. Just like our own homes, by what we think and say.
b. Our human nature gets in the way.
c. Putting a curse on Pastor and others by thought and word, crashing home and church.
d. Simple as that, but not easy.

WE WILL REALIZE WE ARE THE PROBLEM

a Do we want Revival or not?
b. Is the price of dying out to self too much, to go after something that is already won for us?

RECONIZING GOD GIVEN AUTHORITY

a. Letting your Pastor be the leader.
b. What to do if he is wrong.
c. Learning to trust God.
d. How to pray for your pastor.

ARE THERE BULLIES IN THE CHURCH?

a. Who want to rule the Pastor and church?
b. What is your attitude about that?
c. Prayers that set them and the church free.
d. Bless, so you will receive a blessing.

Summary: Where the people change, the church will change. You can have the church you want. Revival is within reach. It begins with you.

"Forgive
Their Sins
And
Heal their
Land"
Our
Country

HOW DO WE PRAY FOR OUR COUNTRY?

The enemy has come into our country
On every side like a flood.
We have prayed and we have not seen answers.
Many Christians think there is no answer, but all is not lost.

11 Corth 10:4-5 KJV (For the weapons of our warfare are not carnal, but mighty through God to the pulling down of strongholds:) casting down imaginations and every high thing that exalted itself against the knowledge of God, and bringing into captivity every thought to the obedience of Christ. Bring our thoughts to align with what the Word says is already ours or is God's will for us. It is a warfare and not easy." I will no more have my mind on the enemy, but You and Your Word"

AT THE END OF 2008

The Lord told the intercessors
How He wanted them to pray
And to believe that God has given
Us the victory, even though it does not look like it.

ISRAEL WAS TO GO INTO THE PROMISED LAND

But the scouts came back with a bad report.
The Enemy was a bigger army, there were high walls,
Giants, and they were better equipped.

THE PEOPLE BELIEVED THE BAD REPORT

Which was true. They were filled with fear.
But God said, "You despised me
Because you would not believe I would be with you."

HE KILLED SPIES WHO GAVE THE BAD REPORT.

None of Israel's adults would go into the Promised Land.
Forty years later, their children went in.
They had learned their lesson.
And God caused them to win battle after battle
Even though the odds were against them.

THE LESSON WE NEED TO LEARN IN THIS CRISIS IS

Fear not, for our God will take us through this
If we believe Him to do this and don't fuss and whine
But are strong and of good courage.

WHAT SHOULD OUR PRAYERS BE LIKE?

Songs of victory, reminding God of His promises;
Having our face before Him as never before.

Psalms 37:4 Delight thyself in the Lord and He shall give you the desires of your heart."
Psalms 34:9 The Message Worship God if you want the best; worship opens the door to all His goodness.

Psams 31:19 The Message What a stack of blessings You have piled up for those who worship You.

THREE ARMIES CAME TO DEFEAT JUDAH.

God told the King where the enemy was
And to march and to put
Praisers in front of the army.

WHEN THEY GOT TO THE ENEMY,

God had put the enemy in confusion
And they had killed each other.
Judah did not even have to fight.

WHEN GOD SEES US PRAISING HIM,

Trusting Him that He has brought us the victory,
We will see a mighty victory for our nation.

WHEN DARK BURDENS COME UPON OUR COUNTRY

Let that be a signal to start praising the Lord.
Praise is a weapon for victory.
Set aside more time for the Lord.

WE ARE IN A SPIRITUAL BATTLE

And we do not fight the enemy
But we respond in a way that
God fights our battles for us.

"I will no more have my mind on the enemy, but on you and your Word."

JUST AS WE NEED TO KEEP

The dark thoughts out of our minds.
Just as the dark thoughts and words
Produce negative results in our homes,
So it is with our country.

PRAYING FOR LEADERS

WHEN BILL CLINTON WAS PRESIDENT,
The Christians were upset about his lifestyle
And they would pray for him out of their anger and disgust.

THE PASTORS IN OUR TOWN
Were joining to pray for revival
And were having their first retreat.
They invited Ruth to attend as an intercessor.

THE SPEAKER SAID THAT
As he spoke around the country,
The intercessors would tell him
That God said to tell the people,

HE CANNOT ANSWER THEIR PRAYERS
For President Clinton
Because people were so offended
They were cursing him in prayer
With all the negatives they were praying.

GOD TOLD THEM IF THEY WOULD
Bless President Clinton
Instead of cursing him,
God would be able to do
A great work in His life.

AND THEN GOD WOULD CAUSE A
A wonderful blessing to fall
Upon our whole country.

AS YOU CAN SEE,
That message never got through.
We, as a country, missed our blessing.

RUTH SPOKE AT CINCINNATI TRANSFORMATION.
She related this story.
After her talk, the speaker before her
Told her that he had lived in Washington, DC
During the Clinton Administration
And he was part of a prayer group
That prayed only for the President.
And yes, they did curse him in prayer.

DURING WORLD WAR II,

Hitler was storming through Europe
Winning country after country.
There seemed to be no stopping him.

FIVE MEN CAME TOGETHER

To pray and ask the Lord,
"How should we pray for Hitler?"

GOD'S ANSWER:

"Pray love for him." "WHAT?
How could we tell people that,
When in our country we all hated him?"

ANSWER: "WE WILL TELL THE INTERCESSORS."

From that day on,
Hitler started to make bad judgments.

HITLER WAS LED BY AN OCCULT BEING,

Could it be that praying love
Cut his connection with that being
And now he was like any other man?
He lost the war.

MY HUSBAND DAN

Fought in World War II in Europe.
When he heard this story
He said "Yes, I know when Hitler
Lost his ability and power
To make judgments as before."

WHEN WE BLESS,

Then God comes down
And is able to set people free
From the powers of darkness
That are working in their lives.

WHEN WE CURSE,

Then people continue to be bound
By those destructive powers.

1 Peter 3:9 Not rendering evil for evil, or railing for railing, but contrary wise blessing, knowing that ye are there unto called, that ye should inherit a blessing.

HOW TO WIN THE VICTORY

WHEN THE ENEMY COMES IN LIKE A FLOOD
Overwhelming us on every side,
How does a standard get raised against the enemy?

WHEN RUTH FIRST WAS TO GO OVERSEAS,
A friend said, "You cannot go,
For you do not know how to fight the devils."

RUTH REPLIED,
"You're right, I don't know how to fight devils,
But I have the invitation to go
And the money to go, so I am going."

SOME MONTHS BEFORE, I HAD MADE A
"Victory Over the Enemy" page
In my Prayer Strategy Resource Book
For a friend who was going through a court trial.
I prayed the page daily for her.

I NOTICED THAT IN THE PAGE,
There were no scriptures
That said I had to fight the devils.
I called the woman and told her that
While overseas, I did not find any devils to fight.

BUT THERE WERE SCRIPTURES ON THAT PAGE
Telling what I had to do to get my answers,
Giving me instructions on what my focus should be
When the enemy came in.
We will go over some of these.

I hide myself in You, Lord, and You protect me from trouble while You surround me with songs of deliverance. You instruct me and teach me in the way I should go. You counsel me and watch over me. Psalm 32:7-8 NIV
I no longer have my mind on the enemy, but stay my mind on You and Your Word. Isaiah 10:20 KJV

WHAT IS OUR BATTLE?
Hiding ourselves in God.
Taking our minds off the enemy.
Staying our minds on God and His Word.

Psalms 91:1,2 He that abideth in the secret place of the most High shall abide under the shadow of the almighty. I will say of the Lord, He is my refuge, my fortress: My God; in Him will I trust.

OTHER SCRIPTURAL INSTRUCTIONS:

We are to say words about God,
Not about the enemy,
But all about what and Who God is.

Below From "Victory Over the Enemy" page
No weapon formed against me succeeds. Isaiah 54:17

I have nothing to fear, for You, Lord, are with me. I do not look around with terror, and I am not dismayed, for You are my God. You have strengthened me to difficulties. Yes, You are helping me, holding me up and retaining me with Your victorious right hand of rightness and justice. Isaiah 41:10

Thank You, God, You have given me the victory through my Lord Jesus Christ. 1 Corth. 15: 57

I am not afraid of the battle ahead, for the battle is not mine, but Yours, God. I need not fight, but stand still and see that Your salvation is now with me. 2 Chron. 20:15b, 17a

The battle is not theirs, but God's to fight.
The battle was ahead of them.
Their part was to stand still and see God fight for them.
They believed they now had the victory (before the battle).

Psalm 148: 6-9 With the high praises of God in their mouths, and a twoedged sword (Word of God) in their hand; To execute vengeance upon the heathen, and punishment upon the people; To bind their Kings with chains, and their nobles with fetters of iron; To execute upon them the judgment written: this honor have all the saints.

GOD DESTROYED SOME OF HIS PEOPLE

When they fussed, whined and complained.
But we, with the high praises in our mouths,
Going forth with the Word of God,
Destroy the enemy.
Let us bring forth with rejoicing.
Do we want to win? Let us go to work.

SOME FEEL LED TO PRAY THE FOLLOWING PAGES

From Prayer Strategy Resource Book.

VICTORY OVER THE ENEMY

1. In these days, no weapon formed against our country succeeds, and we have justice against every lie, for this is our heritage. This is the blessing You have given us, for we are Your servants. Isaiah 54:17 TLB But in that coming day, no weapon turned against you shall succeed, and you will have justice against every courtroom lie. This is the heritage of the servants of the Lord. This is the blessing I have given you," says the Lord.

2. We have nothing to fear, for You, Lord, are with us. We do not look around with terror and we are not dismayed, for You are our God. You have strengthened us to difficulties. Yes, You are helping us, holding us up and retaining us with Your victorious right hand of rightness and justice. Isaiah 41:10 AMP Fear not [there is nothing to fear], for I am with you; do not look around in terror and be dismayed, for I am your God. I will strengthen and harden you to difficulties, yes, I will help you; yes I will hold you up and retain you with my [victorious] right hand of rightness and justice.

3. We hide ourselves in You, Lord, and You protect us from trouble while You surround us with songs of deliverance. You instruct us and teach us in the way we should go. You counsel us and watch over us. Psalm 32:7-8 NIV You are my hiding place; you will protect me from trouble and surround me with songs of deliverance. I will instruct you and teach you in the way you should go; I will counsel you and watch over you.

4. God, You always cause us to triumph in Christ. 2 Corth. 2:14a KJV Now thanks be unto God, which always causeth us to triumph in Christ.

5. We no longer have our minds on the enemy, but stay our minds on You and Your Word. Isaiah 10:20 KJV And it shall come to pass in that day, that the remnant of Israel, and such as are escaped of the house of Jacob, shall no more again stay upon him that smote them; but shall stay upon the LORD, the Holy One of Israel, in truth.

6. Lord, You have preserved us from all evil. Psalm 121:7 KJV The LORD shall preserve thee from all evil: he shall preserve thy soul.

7. We love You, Lord, for You have heard our prayers and answered them. Psalm 116:1 TLB I love the Lord because he hears my prayers and answers them.

8. Thank You, God, You have given us the victory through our Lord Jesus Christ. 1 Corth. 15:57 KJV But thanks *be* to God, which giveth us the victory through our Lord Jesus Christ.

9. You, Lord, are our strength. You teach our hands to war and our fingers to fight. You are our goodness, our fortress, our high

tower, our deliverer, our shield; and in You, we put our trust. You subdue the people under us. Psalms 144:1-2 KJV Blessed be the LORD my strength, which teacheth my hands to war, and my fingers to fight: My goodness, and my fortress; my high tower, and my deliverer; my shield, and he in whom I trust; who subdueth my people under me.

10. Our adversaries are clothed with shame and they cover themselves with their own confusion. Psalm 109:29 KJV Let mine adversaries be clothed with shame, and let them cover themselves with their own confusion, as with a mantle.

11. You have delivered us from wicked and evil men who are not believers. 2 Thes. 3:2 NIV And pray that we may be delivered from wicked and evil men, for not everyone has faith.

12. You have made perfect everything that concerns us, for we are the work of Your hands. Psalm 138:8 KJV The LORD will perfect that which concerneth me: thy mercy, O LORD, endureth forever: forsake not the works of thine own hands.

13. Your angels have camped all around our country and have delivered us. Psalm 34:7 NKJV The angel of the LORD encamps all around those who fear Him, And delivers them.

14. Lord, we trust in You alone and enemies do not defeat us. You rescue us because You always do right. Psalm 31:1 TLB Lord, I trust in you alone. Don't let my enemies defeat me. Rescue me because you are the God who always does what is right.

15. We are not afraid of the battle ahead, for the battle is not ours, but Yours, God. We need not fight, but stand still and see that Your salvation is now with us. 2 Chron. 20:15b,17a KJV Be not afraid nor dismayed by reason of this great multitude; for the battle is not yours, but God's. Ye shall not need to fight in this battle: set yourselves, stand ye still, and see the salvation of the LORD with you.

16. God, You said, "I will never fail you nor forsake you." So we say without fear or doubt, "You, Lord, are our helper. We are not afraid of anything that mere man can do to us." Hebrews 13:5a-6 TLB God has said, "I will never, never fail you nor forsake you." That is why we can say without any doubt or fear, "The Lord is my Helper, and I am not afraid of anything that mere man can do to me."

17. We make our ways to please You, God, so now our worst enemies are at peace with us. Proverbs 16:7 TLB When a man is trying to please God, God makes even his worst enemies to be at peace with him.

(Excerpts from Prayer Strategy Resource Book)

PRAYER FOR THOSE IN AUTHORITY

1. We pray for Your highest will for others, Lord, especially for our leaders, and we thank You for all You are doing for them through our prayers. Because of these prayers, we are able to live in peace and quiet, thinking much about You. 1 Timothy 2:1-2 TLB Here are my directions: Pray much for others; plead for God's mercy upon them; give thanks for all he is going to do for them. Pray in this way for kings and all others who are in authority over us, or are in places of high responsibility, so that we can live in peace and quietness, spending our time in godly living and thinking much about the Lord.

2. Our prayer for our leaders is that they now respect and fear You, Lord, so that now they have wisdom and hate the evil of pride, arrogance, corruption, and deceit of every kind. Proverbs 8:13 TLB If anyone respects and fears God, he will hate evil. For wisdom hates pride, arrogance, corruption, and deceit of every kind.

3. We believe that because of our prayers, You have turned the thoughts of our leaders' hearts in a way that blesses our country, our city, our churches, and our homes. Proverbs 21:1 TLB Just as water is turned into irrigation ditches, so the Lord directs the king's thoughts. He turns them wherever he wants to.

4. We thank You for the salvation of our leaders. You have heard our prayers and now these leaders rejoice in Your salvation with great strength and joy. Psalm 21:1 KJV The king shall joy in thy strength, O LORD; and in thy salvation how greatly shall he rejoice!

5. Because of our prayers, we believe that our leaders have great glory in Your salvation and that You, Lord, have placed honor and majesty upon them. Psalm 21:5 KJV His glory is great in thy salvation: honour and majesty hast thou laid upon him.

6. You, God, have removed the wicked from before our leaders so they are able to rule in a spiritual and moral righteousness in every area and relation. Proverbs 25:5 AMP Take away the wicked from before the king, and his throne will be established in righteousness, spiritual and moral rectitude in every area and relation.

7. Thank You for cutting off the strength of evil leaders and increasing the power of good men in their places. Psalm 75:10 TLB "I will cut off the strength of evil men," says the Lord, "and increase the power of good men in their place."

8. I obey those who have the rule over me and submit to them. Hebrews 13:17 KJV Obey them that have the rule over you, and submit yourself.

9. We believe that our leaders have turned about face. You have revised their lives. Look, You are already pouring Your spirit upon them; You tell them all You know. Proverbs 1:23 MES About face! I can revise your life. Look, I'm ready to pour out my spirit on you; I'm ready to tell you all I know.

10. Jesus, You have spoiled the principalities and the powers of the devil and we agree that these powers are now bound over our country, our government, our cities, our churches, our ministries and our families. We declare Jesus' Lordship. Col. 2:15 KJV And having spoiled principalities and powers, he made a shew of them openly, triumphing over them in it. 1 John 3:8 KJV For this purpose the Son of God was manifested, that he might destroy the works of the devil.

11. We rejoice that our leaders in our government and people in our country have repented, that their sins are now blotted out, and that times of refreshing and revival have come from Your presence, Lord. Acts 3:19 KJV Repent ye therefore, and be converted, that your sins may be blotted out, when the times of refreshing shall come from the presence of the Lord.

12. We thank You for raising up godly men and women to rule over us. Psalm 75:6-7 The Book For promotion and power come from nowhere on earth, but only from God. He promotes one and deposes another.

13. Our leaders trust in You, Lord. Your unfailing love keeps them from stumbling. Psalm 21:7 NLT For the king trust in the Lord. The unfailing love of the Most High will keep him from stumbling.

14. We pray that our President lives close to You forever, Lord. We believe You have sent out Your loving kindness and truth to guard and watch over him. Psalm 61:7 TLB And I shall live before the Lord forever. Oh, send your loving-kindness and truth to guard and watch over me.

15. Our prayer is that You now have filled the leaders of our country with the knowledge of Your will in all wisdom and spiritual understanding; and that they are walking worthy of You Lord unto all pleasing, being fruitful in every good work and increasing in the knowledge of God; strengthened with all might according to your glorious power, unto all patience and longsuffering with joyfulness. Colossians 1:9-11 We do not cease to pray for you, and to desire that ye may be filled with the knowledge of his will in all wisdom and spiritual understanding; that ye may walk worthy of the Lord unto all pleasing, being fruitful in every good work, and increasing in the knowledge of God; Strengthened with all might, according to His glorious power, unto all patience and longsuffering with joyfulness.

Excerpts from Prayer Strategy Resource Books

BRINGING UNITY

1. We speak the same thing in our country and there is no division among us, but we are perfectly joined together in the same mind and the same judgment. 1 Corth. 1:10 KJV Now I beseech you, brethren, by the name of our Lord Jesus Christ, that ye all speak the same thing, and that there be no divisions among you; but that ye be perfectly joined together in the same mind and in the same judgment.

2. Thank You, God, You have helped us to live with patience and harmony with each other with Christ-like attitudes, so we praise You with one voice, giving You glory. We now receive each other warmly as Christ received us, so You are glorified. Romans 15:5-7 KJV Now the God of patience and consolation grant you to be like-minded one toward another according to Christ Jesus: That ye may with one mind and one mouth glorify God, even the Father of our Lord Jesus Christ. Wherefore receive ye one another, as Christ also received us to the glory of God.

3. Because we refresh ourselves in Your presence, Lord, we have such joy and fellowship with each other and are able to stay free of sin. 1 John 1:7 TLB But if we are living in the light of God's presence, just as Christ does, then we have wonderful fellowship and joy with each other, and the blood of Jesus his Son cleanses us from every sin.

4. Thank You, Jesus, that You are our way of peace. You have broken down the enemy's wall that separated us. You have made all of us who opposed each other in our country parts of You, and in that way, we have become one. Ephes 2:14 AMP For he himself is our peace - our bond of unity and harmony. He has made us both one (body) and broken down (destroyed, abolished) the hostile dividing wall between us, by abolishing in his own (crucified) flesh the enmity (caused by) the law with its decrees and ordinances - which He annulled: that he from the two might create in Himself one new quality of humanity out of the two - so making peace.

5. We are encouraged in heart and united in love in our country, so that we now have the full riches of complete understanding, so that we know the mystery of God, namely You, Jesus. Col. 2:2 NIV My purpose is that they may be encouraged in heart and united in love, so that they may have the full riches of complete understanding, in order that they may know the mystery of God, namely, Christ.

6. We now keep the unity of the spirit in a bond of peace. Ephes. 4:3 KJV Endeavoring to keep the unity of the Spirit in the bond of peace.

7. We are like one happy family, full of sympathy toward each other, loving one another with tender hearts and humble minds. 1 Peter 3:8 TLB And now this word to all of you: You should be like one big happy family, full of sympathy toward each other, loving one another with tender hearts and humble minds.

8. We are brothers in You, Lord, sharing the same Spirit. Our hearts are tender and sympathetic to each other. We love each other, agreeing wholeheartedly with each other, working together with one heart and mind and purpose. Philip. 2:1b The Book Does it mean anything to you that we are brothers in the Lord sharing the same Spirit? Are your hearts tender and sympathetic at all? Then make me truly happy by loving each other and agreeing wholeheartedly with each other, working together with one heart and mind and purpose.

9. Thank You, Jesus, we are all one as You and the Father are one. People see this and they believe that You, God, sent Jesus. John 17:21 KJV That they all may be one; as thou, Father, art in me, and I in thee, that they also may be one in us: that the world may believe that thou hast sent me.

10. We have risen and are shining. Our light, which is You, Jesus, has come and Your glory has risen upon us. Isaiah 60:1 KJV Arise, shine; for thy light is come, and the glory of the LORD is risen upon thee.

11. Thank You that You have made our love to grow and overflow to each other and to all men. 1 Thes. 3:12 KJV And the Lord make you to increase and abound in love one toward another, and toward all men, even as we do toward you.

12. It is good and pleasant that we now dwell in unity! Because of our unity, You have commanded a blessing on us, even life forever more. Psalm 133:1,3b KJV Behold, how good and how pleasant it is for brethren to dwell together in unity: for there the LORD commanded the blessing, even life for evermore.

13. I welcome fellow believers who don't see things the way I do, being strong on opinions but weak in faith. I treat them gently. Romans 14:1 MES Welcome with open arms fellow believers who don't see things the way you do. And don't jump all over them when they do or say something you don't agree with—even when it seems they are strong in opinions and weak in the faith department. Remember they have their own history to deal with. Treat them gently.

14. We believers in our country now agree with one heart and one mind. Acts 4:32a NIV All the believers were one in heart and mind.

15. Lord, You have given us one heart and mind to do Your commandments. 2 Chron. 30:12 KJV In Judah the hand of the Lord was to give them one heart to do the commandments of the king and of the princes, by the word of the Lord.

16. The Glory which God gave You, Jesus, You have given to us, so we are now one, even as You and the Father are one. John 17:22 KJV And the glory which thou gavest me I have given them; that they be made one even as we are one.

Books and Resource

PRAYER STRATEGY RESOURCE BOOK: Individual topics for each page. Pick out what you need or desire. Jesus has already won it all for you and is waiting to activate it into your life and the lives of others. Large size 8x11.5, 80 pages. Small size 5.5x8, 80 pages. **Also on CD**

UNLOCKING THE HEAVENS: Step-by-step story of how Ruth learned scriptural strategy to *Unlock the Heavens* for her.

HOW TO GET A MATE AND KEEP'EM Prayers that work. Skills:Where you change, you change the environment around you, building relationships.

SEEDS OF REVIVAL: II Chronicles 7:14, each segment. Discovering sin in our inner nature. Skills in prayers that work.

MIRACLE FAMILY PRAYER BOOK: Families agreeing together in prayer, allowing them to flourish in God's love and blessing.

PRAYING IN YOUR FUTURE: Prayer focus for each day of the week, or you can pray the whole book. Good for teens. 5x7 Pamphlet

PRAYING FOR YOUR CITY: Prayer for each day. Believing prayers of great joy for city revival.

FEAR NOT: Jewish prayer book, 4"x51/2" with 18 pages. Scriptures from Jewish Scripture books.

WE DECLARE – FOR ISRAEL: Promises for Israel, formatted into believing prayers. Scriptures from Jewish Bible. 5 X 8.

LIVING WATERS: CASSETTE TAPE. Ruth reading the prayers. Son David Shinness playing the clarinet and son Tom Shinness playing the guitar for background for the prayers. Worship hymns.

PRAYING IN YOUR FUTURE: CASSETTE TAPE. Ruth reading the prayers from the Praying In Your Future book. Son Tom Shinness playing different stringed instruments of hymns in background.

SCRIPTURAL PRAYERS WITH MUSIC: CD containing the two cassettes above.

UNLOCKING THE HEAVENS DVD SEMINAR: Four hours long. Four Topics: Testimony, How to Raise Up Your Heart and Home, How To Pray in Your Own Ministry, Testimonies.

PRAYER STRATEGY RESOURCE BOOK CD: Ruth reading the prayers and son Tom Shinness accompanying with guitar.

To obtain additional copies of this material, please write or call or e-mail
Ruth Shinness-Brinduse
2539 E. 450 N. Anderson, IN 46012-9518 Ph: 765-643-0612
E-mail: PrayerStrategy@juno.com Web page: www.prayerstrategy.com